CAMPING

by Tim Seeberg

Content Adviser: Cathy Scheder,
Manager of Learning Resources,
American Camping Association,
Martinsville, Indiana

Published in the United States of America by The Child's World®
PO Box 326 • Chanhassen, MN 55317-0326 • 800-599-READ • www.childsworld.com

Acknowledgments

The Child's World®: Mary Berendes, Publishing Director

Editorial Directions, Inc.: E. Russell Primm, Editorial Director; Halley Gatenby, Line Editor; Susan Hindman, Copyeditor; Elizabeth K. Martin and Katie Marsico, Assistant Editors; Matthew Messbarger, Editorial Assistant; Peter Garnham, Christine Simms, and Kathy Stevenson, Fact Checkers; Tim Griffin/IndexServ, Indexer; James Buckley Jr., Photo Researcher and Photo Selector

The Design Lab: Kathleen Petelinsek, Design and Art Production

Photos

Cover: Getty Images.
Corbis: 5, 8, 14, 15.
Lee Cohen/Corbis: 12, 24; Layne Kennedy/Corbis: 11, 16, 26; Buddy Mays/Corbis: 21; Jim McDonald: 28; Joel Rogers/Corbis: 7; George Shelley/Corbis: 19; Ariel Skelley: 25; Scott Smith/Corbis: 22; Karl Weatherly/Corbis: 17.

Library of Congress Cataloging-in-Publication Data

Seeberg, Tim.
  Camping / by Tim Seeberg.
    p. cm. — (Kids' guides)
  Summary: An introduction to camping, describing different kinds of camping, how to plan a camping trip, equipment needed, safety concerns, and more.
  Includes bibliographical references (p.   ) and index.
   ISBN 1-59296-032-4 (lib. bdg. : alk. paper)
   1. Camping—Juvenile literature. [1. Camping.] I. Title. II. Series.
  GV191.7.S44 2004
  796.54—dc22   2003017801

CONTENTS

INTO THE WOODS

HAVE YOU EVER BEEN CAMPING?

If not, you might be wondering what it is like to spend whole days—and nights—outside. Away from your cozy bed and your refrigerator filled with food. On purpose. You are probably curious about what it is like to watch the sun rise and set in a forest, a desert, or the mountains. Or on a sandy beach beside a lake, a river, or an ocean. You might even wonder how people can possibly be comfortable and safe outdoors in the wild. How do they play, eat, and sleep without the conveniences of their home or a hotel? And what is there to do all day and night without television, video games, a computer, or the telephone?

If you have been camping, you know it can be fun and exciting. You know what it is to feel like an explorer, surviving without most of our modern luxuries. You remember the challenge of helping to build the campfire. You smile when you think about enjoying the warmth of that fire while gazing up at a sky filled with stars. You laugh when you recall the time you chased a lizard down the trail. Your mouth starts to water as you imagine how delicious all the food was—even the slightly burned hot dogs. And you cannot wait until the next time you get to wrap yourself in your warm sleeping bag and fall asleep to the sounds of nature all around you.

This book will introduce you to camping. You will discover the different types of camping. You will find out how to help your family or friends plan a camping trip. You will learn about the essential equipment and supplies that make a camping trip successful. You will also find out the two most important things about camping—how to have fun and how to be safe.

So, what is camping, anyway? Technically, camping is temporarily living away from urban areas, with tents or other **portable** materials as shelter. But there is much more to camping than that. Camping is sleeping under the stars, listening to crickets chirp, and discovering the fresh smells of nature. Camping is sharing special experiences with family and friends. Camping is getting away from familiar habits and distractions and discovering something new about yourself. Camping is becoming reacquainted with all your senses.

Let's go camping!

Being with your family is one of the best parts of camping.

CHAPTER ONE

PLANNING YOUR ADVENTURE

AFTER YOU HAVE DECIDED THAT YOU

want to go camping, it is time to make your plans. Camping can be exciting, fun, and simple. It also can be frustrating, difficult—even dangerous. However, it does not have to be. The best guarantee of a great camping experience is careful and complete planning. Besides, planning your trip is a big part of the adventure.

What kind of food should you bring? What clothes will you need? Should you have special equipment? What about shelter? What activities will you do? Do you need to be concerned about dangerous animals?

These are excellent questions. Before you can answer them, however, you first have to answer some more basic questions. How many days and nights will you be camping? Who will be camping with you? Will you stay at one campsite or move to different sites? Will you have a car nearby? What will the weather be like? The answers to these questions will determine the answers to almost all other questions you have about going camping.

First, decide how long to camp. You might feel comfortable spending a weekend away from your bed and the microwave. However, are you ready to be out there for a week? Whether you will be camping with family or friends, discuss everyone's expec-

tations ahead of time. Campers who expect to relax at camp may not mix well with campers who want to be active.

Many people camp in the woods, but beaches can make great campsites, too.

For your first few trips, practice your camping skills closer to home and in well-traveled areas. It takes years to become a camping and wilderness expert.

An important part of your planning is knowing what weather to expect. Choose a season when your tent is least likely to be flooded by rain. Even in dry seasons, check weather forecasts immediately before your trip. Always be prepared for the unexpected.

Some camp-
grounds have
permanent
tents for camp-
ers to use.

As you complete your plan, contact park officials at your destination. They can inform you about unseasonable weather and other local news. They can also tell you about campsites, reservations, fees, activities, and rules. Most campgrounds also have Web sites that provide the information you will need.

Your plan should include a budget, which means how much money you will need to spend. If money is tight, you can still have a fantastic camping trip. Just do not go as far away—or as far into the wilderness. The farther out you go, the more specialized and expensive the equipment you will need. Also, the longer your trip, the more supplies and equipment you will have to bring. Find out about camping fees at your intended destination. And remember to include the cost of getting there, such as gasoline and parking fees.

Deciding where to go camping is lots of fun. Everyone on the trip can suggest ideas about where to go, what to see, and what to do.

There are many kinds of campgrounds. Even within a relatively small area, the **terrain** can vary greatly. Do some research before choosing a site. Divide up the tasks and have everyone check out Web sites for different campgrounds. Look at national parks, state and county parks, and private campgrounds. Then get together and go over what you have found.

Be aware of each campground's **geography** and native plants and animals. Study the plants and creatures, and learn to avoid those that are dangerous or endangered. Find out if you will be camping near a body of water, in a dense forest, on steep mountains, or in a barren desert. Avoid camping near **stagnant** ponds or thick, damp woods; these places are usually filled with insects, such as mosquitoes.

TYPES OF CAMPING

The most common types of camping are backyard camping, backpacking, car camping, and RV camping.

Your first backyard camping trip might be to your own backyard, deck, or balcony. Use a **tarp** for a tent, use blankets for a sleeping bag, and bring a flashlight. If your family has a barbecue grill, that can serve as your stove.

Backpackers carry all their equipment on their backs. They take only what they absolutely need. That usually includes a small tent, a sleeping bag, a backpacker's stove, a cooking pot, and clothes. They also carry dried food and drinking water.

Car campers park their car at or very close to their campsite, so they can bring along more of the comforts of home. They often use a bigger tent, pillows, and an air mattress. They can bring more cooking gear, folding chairs, and ice chests, among other gear. You can car camp at state and national parks and at **commercial** campgrounds.

RV stands for recreational vehicle, such as a pickup truck with a **camper shell** or an all-in-one motor home. RVs often include a bed, a stove, and a refrigerator, and sometimes even a shower and a toilet.

The information you gather about the campsites will help you organize your clothing, gear, and first-aid kit. For example, if you are going to poisonous snake country, you should pack a snakebite kit. For your first few camping trips, look for campgrounds with safe water supplies, showers, and bathrooms. The more comfortable you become with your camping skills, the more you might want to rough it the next time. Don't force yourself to do too much, too soon.

CHAPTER TWO

GETTING READY TO GO

ONCE YOU HAVE AN IDEA OF WHERE

you would like to go, you can plan what to take. Use the suggestions in this chapter as a guide, but make sure your own list includes everything you will need and want—and nothing you will not.

The first rule of packing for a camping trip is to pack smart. Make a list of what to bring. Pack clothes that are not too bulky or too heavy to carry, especially if you are backpacking. When you pack to go camping, the most important question is the weather. Is there a chance it will rain? Will it be really hot? Really cold? Although you can listen to the weather forecast before you leave your house, you can still get caught in an unexpected rain shower or heat wave. Plus, temperatures at many campsites can range from freezing in the morning

Planning your camping trip sometimes means lining up all your gear to make sure you've got what you need.

Sturdy boots are important, especially if you plan on making hikes from your campsite.

to very hot in the daytime. Be prepared for changes in weather.

For most situations, clothes made of cotton, such as T-shirts and jeans, work well. They are comfortable and lightweight. Cotton does absorb moisture, though, so it is not a good material in wet or cold weather. If you expect to experience these kinds of conditions, you will be more comfortable in clothing made from **synthetic** fabrics.

Regardless of the forecast, it makes sense to bring along a lightweight jacket and a warm hat. In chilly weather, the key to keeping warm is to conserve your body's natural heat. Because people lose most of their body heat from their head, a wool, fleece, or **acrylic** hat is one of the most important items to pack.

Expect to do a lot of walking when you are camping. Even if you do not have to hike to your campsite, explore the area around it. Do yourself a huge favor and bring good-quality socks. These will support and protect your feet. They also will keep them dry and comfortable.

Good shoes are equally important. If you are planning nothing more than short hikes on gentle trails, a good pair of sneakers will work well. In warmer weather, especially if you are planning water activities, it is a good idea to bring water-proof sandals. Hiking boots are better for longer hikes. They are sturdy, support your ankles, and absorb shock. If you go shopping for boots, make sure they fit properly. Try on the boots with the socks you will be wearing on your trip. Your feet should fit snugly—but not tightly—in the boots. If your feet can move around at all inside the boot—other than being able to wiggle your toes—you will get blisters and quickly become very uncomfortable.

When planning a camping trip, bring a variety of foods that are easy to store and keep fresh. Dried fruits and trail mix are yummy munchies on the trail. You can even make your own trail mix.

Many books and Web sites offer simple and delicious recipes for food you can make at home to take along. Always pack your food in sealed containers. Prior to packing, measure and combine dry ingredients in zip-locked bags. Label each bag so you know which meal it is for. Keep food properly cooled in an insulated and sealed container. You may want to bring a **grate** to put over the fire. Not every campsite has a grill that will suit your cooking needs.

Everything—even spaghetti—tastes better when it's cooked outdoors!

ESSENTIAL EQUIPMENT

One of the great things about camping is you can do it with very little gear. The type of camping trip you plan will determine what you bring. For almost all camping trips, however, the list below includes the most important things you should pack.

- compass (learn how to use it before you leave home)
- emergency candle (in case you lose or break your flashlight)
- emergency whistle (keep it in your pocket, attached to a zipper, or on a cord around your neck and use it *only* in an emergency—if you are lost, for instance)
- first-aid kit (a waterproof bag or container filled with moist towelettes, bandages, gauze and adhesive tape, small scissors, blister patches, and aspirin)
- flashlight (with extra batteries)
- insect repellent
- maps
- matches (stored in a canister or container that will allow them to stay dry)
- nylon cord (for a clothesline or to hang food in trees out of reach of animals)
- plastic garbage bags (for collecting trash, for dirty clothes, and for emergency rain protection)
- safety pins, needle, and thread
- sunscreen
- toilet paper
- trowel or small shovel (to dig a pit toilet and a food scrap hole)
- water filter or water purifying tablets
- water jug

FIRST AID KIT

You can camp in all sorts of weather—just make sure to plan ahead!

Before you leave, tell your exact plans to someone close to you, such as a neighbor or a friend. If something goes wrong and you don't return on time, this person can tell authorities where to find you quickly.

You are smart to have a plan. Remember, though, you can't plan for everything. You may not be able to pick your campsite. The weather may change drastically. Some of your experience will depend on luck. Most of it, however, will depend on your attitude, your creativity, and your preparation. Camping is an adventure, and the most important thing you can bring along is your ability to make the best of every situation.

CHAPTER THREE

HOME, SWEET . . . CAMPSITE

YOU HAVE MADE YOUR PLANS AND

completed all your preparations. Whether by car, by boat, or by

foot, you have arrived at that area where you will camp. Now

you are ready to establish your new home away from home.

The excitement at this point is wonderful. You will be

eager to settle in to your campsite: pitch your tent, find the

Once you've found
your campsite, get
your tent set up in
a safe location.

swimming hole, build the campfire, have a snack, meet your new neighbors (people *and* wildlife), set up the "kitchen," play hide-and-seek. Let the fun begin!

Actually, the fun *has* begun. And it will continue if you stick to your plan. So, before you do any of those things you are so keen to do, choose the best spot to make camp. Together with the rest of your group, walk around the area. **Familiarize** yourself with your surroundings. Find the best source for water. Locate level, high ground that will not get flooded in a surprise rainstorm. Are bathrooms located nearby? Should you be closer to that giant pine tree or farther away from it? Is that a hornets' nest hanging from that branch? Does a trail run right through here? With careful observation, your group should be able to decide fairly quickly where to make camp.

Now is a great time to divide responsibilities. Whenever possible, work together. Teamwork makes camping easier and more fun. Some people can pitch the tents and lay out bedrolls and sleeping bags. Others can build the fire ring. Still others can gather firewood and water. If possible, do all these things before the sun sets. Setting up camp is much easier in the daylight.

The campfire is one of the best parts of camping. The scent of wood smoke, the glowing **embers,** and the dance of the flames are all beautiful. So, too, are the stories and laughter

A roaring fire on a starry night is part of the best times on a camping trip.

shared there with friends and family. Many of your favorite camping memories will probably center on the campfire. But be careful! Read the campfire safety tips in the box on the following page, and always follow them carefully.

CAMPFIRE SAFETY

The campfire requires more caution and attention than any other aspect of camping. Follow these tips to be safe and responsible with your campfire:

- Before you build a campfire, be sure campfires are allowed. Check before you leave home, and then double-check with the campground manager or forest ranger when you arrive. He or she can also show you how to build a safe and enjoyable campfire.
- If your campsite does not already have a fire ring, build one to ensure your fire remains under control. Build the ring on dirt—not on dead leaves, weeds, or moss—in an open area with a clear view of the sky. Make it large enough for your fire, plus leave several feet of open space for safety. You may want to surround your fire ring with rocks for extra protection.
- Never start a campfire before you have water on hand to put it out.
- Never leave a campfire unattended.
- Burn only dry wood lying on the ground or wood you brought with you. Do not cut down live trees or cut branches from trees near the campsite.
- Collect firewood far away from your campsite, so the camping area will not look bare and unnatural.
- Extinguish all fires by pouring water on them, stirring the ashes, and then pouring on more water. Ashes should be cool to the touch before you leave.
- Pick out any trash that is not completely burned to ash.
- If you have any extra split wood, leave some behind. It will be a wonderful surprise for the next campers who arrive at the campsite.

Campfire food always tastes great. Whether you cook hot dogs and baked beans or a fancy steak and potato dinner—or even a bowl of oatmeal for breakfast—you will be amazed at how delicious everything is.

A hearty stew can be an easy and tasty camping meal.

Some campers enjoy making elaborate meals in the humble setting of their campsite. Others just want to eat simply. That gives them more time to hike, fish, or play games. Everyone has their own style. However you approach campsite cooking, these tips will probably help you.

Meals that can be cooked at home and that travel well in a cooler will save a lot of time, especially for the first night of your trip. Precooked meat lasts longer in the cooler than raw meat.

Bring cooking and cleanup supplies from home. Pot

Hanging food from trees helps keep animals from finding a midnight snack.

holders and an oven mitt will help during the cooking and are useful around the campfire. A sponge with a scrubber on one side makes washing pots and dishes easier. A hand-cranking can opener can save you a lot of effort! Make your cookout—and cleanup— a group activity.

If you are camping in bear country, hang your trash bag high off the ground and a good distance from your tent at night. If you're staying at an established campground, place your bag in the special bearproof receptacles at night.

S'MORES:
EVERYONE'S FAVORITE CAMPFIRE FOOD

Without a doubt, the best campfire treats in the world are those sticky, gooey, yummy creations called S'Mores. They are quick, easy, and fun to make.

Ingredients

Large marshmallows

Graham crackers

Chocolate bars

Directions

Your campfire is burning. You've found some long roasting sticks that you've wiped clean or **whittled** the bark off of. (Or you planned ahead and brought some long skewers and extra oven mitts.) Now tear open a bag of large marshmallows and get ready to roast some dessert! Using your roasting stick, hold two marshmallows over the open fire. (Don't hold them too close to the flames or the marshmallows will burn. If they should catch fire, don't panic! Just pull the stick toward you and blow out the flame. They will still be good.) Turn the stick often to heat the marshmallows evenly.

When they are a toasty brown, slide the marshmallows off the stick. (You might want to have an adult help you with this because the marshmallows and the stick will be hot.) Immediately smush the toasted marshmallows onto a graham cracker. Add some pieces of the chocolate bar. Complete the sandwich by putting another graham cracker on top, and gently squeeze it all together. The chocolate melts into the marshmallow, and the creamy goo makes the graham crackers stick together. Open wide and bite into a delicious tradition!

CHAPTER FOUR

KEEPING IT SAFE

CAMPING IS A SAFE AND FUN ACTIVITY

enjoyed by millions of people every year. Major problems are very unlikely, especially when your adventure begins with a good plan. Being aware of safety issues will help even more to keep you from trouble and danger. For your own safety and the safety of others, keep in mind the tips described in this chapter when you are camping.

A great part of any camping trip is making hikes in a nearby forest.

Ah, the old swimming hole! Bring your swimsuit if you'll be near a place to swim.

When you first set up camp, have everyone in the group agree on a place where you will all meet if anyone gets separated from the group. But if you get separated and you are lost, STOP. Find a safe place to sit, and begin blowing your safety whistle. Wait in that spot until someone finds you.

If you leave camp for the day to hike, swim, or do some other activity, be sure to start back well before dark. Remember that daylight hours are shorter in the fall and winter. Take enough food, clothing, and equipment to keep you comfortable

Beautiful lake scenes like this one are often seen on camping trips, but don't drink the water!

in case of an emergency. Be alert to approaching storms, dress properly, and seek appropriate shelter.

Don't drink the water! Rivers, streams, and lakes may be

beautiful, but they contain **microscopic** bugs that can make you very sick if you swallow them. Bring bottled water with you, use water from faucets you know are safe, or use a dependable water purifier.

Do not feed or approach any wildlife, and never corner or challenge a wild animal, including poisonous snakes. If a wild animal does not move away from you, back away slowly. Report sick or aggressive animals to the campground manager or forest ranger. Many areas are affected by **rabies.**

Avoid tick bites by staying on trails and avoiding grassy, brushy areas. Wear light-colored clothing so you can spot ticks more easily. Tuck your shirt into your pants, and tuck your pant legs into your socks. Do not wear shorts on the trails. If a tick is attached to your skin, grab it with tweezers and remove it. Do not crush the tick's body because this can force harmful bacteria into your skin. Wash the bite area thoroughly with soap and water. If you think part of the tick has remained in your skin, or if you think the tick has been attached for longer than 48 hours, get medical attention immediately.

Finally, never leave food in your tent. It can attract animals and insects.

In addition to being aware of safety at all times, you should also be responsible and considerate. As a camper, you are actually a visitor in someone else's home. You are a guest of the wildlife and the natural environment that surround you. Showing appropriate respect and care for your hosts will help to ensure their well-being, as well as your fellow campers'

As the sun sets over a quiet lake, it's time to hit the sleeping bag in your cozy tent.

CAMPING RULES AND REGULATIONS

Many campgrounds post rules to help make people aware of what behavior is appropriate when camping. Always observe posted rules and regulations. If rules are not posted, follow these tips to be a good camper and a good guest.

- If you carry it in, carry it out—this will eliminate litter.
- Protect water sources from **contamination.**
- Use **biodegradable** soap, or try soapless hot-water dishwashing, bathing, and clothes washing.
- When using soap and toothpaste, dispose of the wastewater at least 100 feet (30 meters) away from natural water sources and well- or tap-water sources.
- Control your noise and, if you bring them, your pets.
- Be respectful of the natural environment—keep the trees and shrubs alive and growing.
- Be quiet from 10 P.M. until 6 A.M. Voices and music carry far at night.
- Do not use nails and wires on trees; these can cause them serious damage.
- Clean your campsite before leaving. Leave it as clean as you would want it to be if you were arriving that day.

enjoyment of their experience. Being a good guest is an important part of camping.

The rules listed here and the ones posted at campgrounds may seem like an awful lot of rules to remember. But they really are designed to make everyone's camping experience a good one.

And when you go, save some S'mores for me!

GLOSSARY

acrylic—a chemical used in fibers and paints

biodegradable—capable of being broken down into harmless products

camper shell—a removable unit that fits over the bed of a pickup truck

commercial—something that is run in order to make a profit, such as a business

contamination—the process of making something polluted or dirty

embers—the glowing remains of a fire

familiarize—to study something in order to become accustomed to it or comfortable with it

geography—the physical features of a certain area

grate—a grid made of metal bars that can be placed over an open fire

microscopic—something so tiny that it can only be seen with a magnifying device called a microscope

portable—an object that can be easily moved or carried from place to place

rabies—a disease that infects humans, dogs, and other warm-blooded animals; rabies can cause a person or animal to behave strangely, become paralyzed, or even die

stagnant—a body of water that does not move or flow

synthetic—something that is artificial or man-made

tarp—a piece of material (often plastic) that can be used to cover an area or object

terrain—the ground or landscape

whittled—cut or shaped a stick or piece of wood

FIND OUT MORE

Books

Carlson, Laurie M., and Judith Dammel. *Kids Camp!: Activities for the Backyard or Wilderness.* Chicago: Chicago Review Press, 1995.

Drake, Jane, Ann Love, and Heather Collins (illustrator). *Kids Campfire Book.* Tonawanda, N.Y.: Kids Can Press, 1998.

George, Kristine O'Connell, and Kate Kiesler (illustrator). *Toasting Marshmallows: Camping Poems.* New York: Clarion Books, 2001.

White, Linda, and Fran Lee (illustrator). *Sleeping in a Sack: Camping Activities for Kids.* Salt Lake City: Gibbs-Smith, 1998.

On the Web

Visit our home page for lots of links about camping:
http://www.childsworld.com/links.html

NOTE TO PARENTS, TEACHERS, AND LIBRARIANS: We routinely check our Web links to make sure they're safe, active sites—so encourage your readers to check them out!

INDEX

About the Author

Tim Seeberg is a writer based in Bend, Oregon. He has a lifelong love of the outdoors and is an avid fly fisherman. A graduate of UCLA, Tim has worked in advertising and public relations, and has also written about sports history.